Football Stars

Virginia Buckman
AR B.L.: 5.8 Alt.: 894
Points: 1.0   MG

GREATEST SPORTS HEROES

Football Stars

Virginia Buckman

HIGH
interest
books

Children's Press®
A Division of Scholastic Inc.
New York / Toronto / London / Auckland / Sydney
Mexico City / New Delhi / Hong Kong
Danbury, Connecticut

Book Design: Dean Galiano
Contributing Editor: Jen Silate
Photo credits: cover, pp. 7, 20, 27© Andy Lyons/Getty Images; pp. 4, 14, 17 © Donald Miralle/Getty Images; p. 8 © Stephen Dunn/Getty Images; pp. 11, 28, 31 © Jonathan Daniel/Getty Images; p. 23 © Rick Stewart/Getty Images; p. 24 © Tom Pidgeon/Getty Images; p. 32 © Otto Greule, Jr./Getty Images; p. 37 © Jamie Squire/Getty Images; p. 38 © Jeff Haynes/AFP/Getty Images; p. 41 © Paul Spinelli/Getty Images.

Library of Congress Cataloging-in-Publication Data

Buckman, Virginia.
Football stars/Virginia Buckman.
p. cm.—(Greatest sports heroes)
Includes index.
ISBN-10: 0-531-12586-6 (lib. bdg.)   0-531-18703-9 (pbk.)
ISBN-13: 978-0-531-12586-1 (lib. bdg.)   978-0-531-18703-6 (pbk.)
1. Football players—United States—Biography—Juvenile literature. I. Title. II. Series.

GV939.A1B83 2007
796.332092'2—dc22

2006007148

2 3 4 5 6 7 8 9 10 R 11 10 09 08
                62

Contents

Introduction

"Okay, guys! We've got 30 seconds left in this game. We only need 20 yards to get into field goal range. There's nothing to this." The quarterback gives his offense a wink and breaks the huddle. He knows he just needs to complete one pass to the sidelines to get the 20 yards (18.3 meters) and stop the clock. Then the field goal team can take the field and try for the game-winning field goal.

The quarterback looks across at the defense and senses that they are going to blitz. He knows that with the linebackers coming after him he will have single coverage on his receivers. He calls an audible, a change of play at the line of scrimmage, to take advantage of the defensive coverage.

"Red 42, Red 42!" the quarterback yells. The linebackers fidget, ready to tear across the line and bring him down. "Hike!" The quarterback drops back five steps. The middle

San Diego Chargers fans hold up an "LT" sign to honor their superstar running back LaDainian Tomlinson.

linebacker breaks into the backfield. The quarterback jumps to the left and shakes off the linebacker's tackle. He looks to his left and then to his right. The quarterback feels pressure from his blind side, but he just needs another half second for his receiver to get open. He cocks his arm, looks to the open receiver, and throws the ball a split second before the defensive end takes him down hard to the turf.

As the quarterback hits the ground, he visualizes his receiver grabbing the pass along the right sideline. The quarterback's heart jumps when he hears the roar of the home crowd—a signal that the pass was complete. Now it's the kicker's turn—and there's just time enough to boot the game-winning 3 points!

Professional football provides dozens of thrills such as this in every game. But who are the men who provide these thrills to millions of fans each week? Let's read on to find out more about today's greatest football stars!

Receiver Chad Johnson of the Cincinnati Bengals is congratulated by fans after a win.

Chapter One

Shaun Alexander

On January 6, 2006, Shaun Alexander was voted the National Football League's (NFL) Most Valuable Player (MVP). Being named league MVP was a fitting end to Alexander's incredible season. Shaun led the league in rushing yards and rushing touchdowns as he racked up 1,880 yards (1,719 m) and scored 27 touchdowns. Alexander's heroics led the Seattle Seahawks to the National Football Conference (NFC) West division title and to the 2006 Super Bowl. Yet even with all of his accomplishments, Alexander remains a humble young man.

Early Talent

Shaun Alexander grew up in Florence, Kentucky. People began to notice that he had special talents when he was just a sophomore at Boone County High School. Shaun recalls his coach sitting with him and explaining that

Shaun holds up the NFC Championship trophy after his team's victory over the Carolina Panthers on January 22, 2006.

his future in football was limitless. "It was the first time it hit me that there was something special about me," recalls Alexander. "I just realized, 'Oh. You know what? There is something about me that's special.'"

Senior Success

Shaun posted an incredible 3,166-yard (2,895 m), 54-touchdown season his senior year at Boone County. His remarkable talents earned him a place on the PARADE All-American High School Football Team and the Gatorade Circle of Champions Kentucky Player of the Year

Player Stats

Shaun Alexander

Team: Seattle Seahawks

Position: Running Back

Height: 5' 11"

Weight: 225 lbs.

Born: 8/30/1977

College: Alabama

NFL Experience: 6 years

Shaun gets tackled by the Pittsburgh Steelers defense in Super Bowl XL. The Steelers won the game, 21-10.

award. The college scholarships came rolling in. Teams from all over the country wanted Alexander to play for them. Shaun chose to play for the University of Alabama.

College Ball

During his stellar college career at Alabama, Shaun racked up 3,565 yards (3,259 m) in four seasons. He shattered the previous school mark to become Alabama's all-time leading rusher. He also set school records for 100-yard (91 m) games (15) and rushing touchdowns (41). Alexander was recruited, or scouted, by many NFL teams. He was the nineteenth overall player taken in the first round of the 2000 NFL draft by the Seattle Seahawks.

First-Round Pick

It didn't take long for Shaun to prove his worth in the NFL. After his rookie season, he broke out big time. On October 11, 2001, Shaun shattered a Seahawk record by rushing for 266 yards (243 m) in a single game. He finished his season with an NFL-leading 14 rushing touchdowns. Since 2001, Shaun has been one of the best backs in the NFL.

Helping Others

Shaun is a generous person who likes to share his good fortune with those who are less fortunate. Soon after turning pro, he created the Shaun Alexander Family Foundation, an organization that improves young men's lives by teaching leadership and character.

This allows the young men to develop new interests, achieve goals, and gain valuable knowledge. As Shaun sees it, "I've been blessed, so I want to be a blessing to other people, too."

Sports Trivia

The Top Female Running Back

Most football fans know that Shaun Alexander is the leading rusher in the NFL. Less people know about the leading rusher in the National Women's Football Association (NWFA). Her name is Angela Edwards. Angela rushed for 1,617 yards (1,478 m) in the 2005 season. Angela also scored 27 touchdowns for her team, the West Michigan Mayhem.

Chapter Two

LaDainian Tomlinson

LaDainian Tomlinson is one of the NFL's premier running backs. In just five years in the league, LaDainian has already set the mark as the San Diego Chargers' all-time leading rusher. He has also been selected to the Pro Bowl three times. Tomlinson has rushed for more than 1,000 yards (914 m) in each of his five pro seasons. He is the only player in NFL history to catch 100 passes and rush for more than 1,000 yards in the same season. LaDainian is so well respected in the league that he is simply known by his initials, "LT."

The Early Years

LaDainian grew up in Waco, Texas. As a child, he played Little League football and dreamed of one day playing in the NFL. LaDainian played a few different positions on his high school team, but he did not get a lot of attention from college scouts. Some felt he

LaDainian runs onto the field carrying an American flag in a game against the Dallas Cowboys, on September 11, 2005.

was too small and inexperienced. One college coach who took notice of LaDainian's talent was Pat Sullivan at Texas Christian University. LaDainian was happy to play for TCU since he liked Coach Sullivan and the school was close to his hometown.

TCU

LaDainian had great success at TCU. As a senior he was a Heisman Trophy finalist. He rushed for 5,263 yards (4,812 m) at TCU.

Player Stats

LaDainian Tomlinson

Team: San Diego Chargers

Position: Running Back

Height: 5' 10"

Weight: 221 lbs.

Born: 6/23/1979

College: Texas Christian University (TCU)

NFL Experience: 5 years

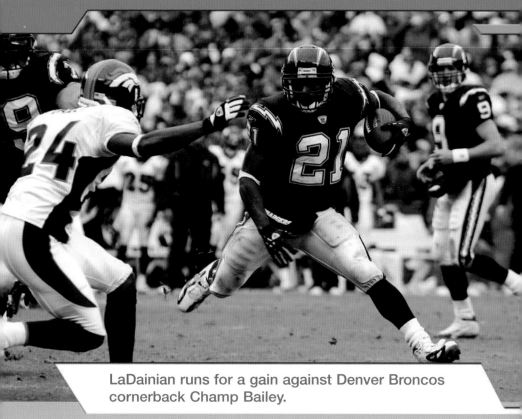

LaDainian runs for a gain against Denver Broncos cornerback Champ Bailey.

LaDainian also set National Collegiate Athletic Association (NCAA) records for most rushing yards in a single game (406) and for most touchdowns in a single game (6).

In 2000, LaDainian won the Doak Walker Award as the nation's top running back and he was selected as an Associated Press All-American his senior year. LaDainian was a superstar NFL prospect coming out of college. He was the fifth overall pick in the 2001 draft.

On the Run

LaDainian was the Chargers' starting running back as a rookie. Since then, he has been one of the top running backs in the league. LaDainian holds the record for most straight games with a rushing touchdown with 18.

On October 16, 2005, LaDainian became only the seventh player in NFL history to run, catch, and throw for a touchdown in the same game.

LaDainian has been called the best running back of all-time by his coach Marty Schottenheimer—and after thirty years of NFL experience, Coach Schottenheimer has seen a lot of the greats.

The Chargers have rewarded LaDainian by signing him to a contract that makes him the highest paid running back in the history of the NFL—more than $60 million for eight years.

Touching Lives

Tomlinson is grateful for his success and he likes to share that success with others in the community. He raises money for his Tomlinson Touching Lives Foundation by hosting charity events. The donations support a college scholarship fund that provides money to needy students. LaDainian also hosts football camps where he personally teaches aspiring athletes about the game.

Fun Fact

Some fans refuse to call LaDainian "LT." They consider the legendary Giants' linebacker Lawrence Taylor the only true "LT." Lawrence Taylor himself has referred to Tomlinson as "BLT," which stands for Baby LT.

Chapter Three

Dwight Freeney

Dwight Freeney is one of the NFL's most feared pass rushers. In his first year in the NFL, Dwight set a rookie record with 9 forced fumbles. He was also runner-up for Defensive Rookie of the Year. Dwight uses his speed and skill to get to the quarterback. Despite his 268-pound (122 kilogram) frame, Dwight has been timed at a speedy 4:48 in the 40-yard (36.6 m) dash.

Becoming a Player

Dwight Freeney was born in Hartford, Connecticut. He did not play organized football until he was a sophomore in high school. Before that, he played football in the street with his friends. "I remember getting tackled into a parked car. If you played street football, it happened to you. You either ran into a mailbox or you fell on the ground and got rocks in your hands. Those were the days."

Dwight applies a crushing tackle on St. Louis Rams running back Steven Jackson.

Dwight played football for Bloomfield High School, where he received PrepStar Magazine All-Regional honors as a defensive end. Dwight also served as team captain of his high school football team.

Star at Syracuse

Dwight was a star at Syracuse University. He was the school's premier pass rusher. He ranks second in school history with 34 sacks. Freeney also holds the NCAA record with 11 forced fumbles in a season. As a senior, he led the nation in sacks with 17.5.

Player Stats

Dwight Freeney

Team: Indianapolis Colts

Position: Defensive End

Height: 6' 1"

Weight: 268 lbs.

Born: 1/4/1978

College: Syracuse University

NFL Experience: 4 years

Dwight powers his way through the Buffalo Bills offensive line in a game won by the Bills, 17-14.

In the NFL

Dwight was a first-round draft pick in 2002. He was the eleventh overall player chosen in the draft. Dwight quickly proved to the Colts that he was worth the first-round pick. In four seasons, he has recorded 51 sacks and 23 forced fumbles. In 2004, he led the NFL with 16 sacks. Dwight's performance earned him a spot in that year's Pro Bowl.

Chad Johnson is considered by many fans to be the best receiver in the NFL today. Chad has posted over 1,000 yards (914 m) receiving in each of the past four seasons. His selection to the 2006 Pro Bowl marked the fourth time in five seasons that Johnson had been honored with that distinction. Johnson averages almost 15 yards (13.7 m) per catch. When asked how he thought a cornerback could best cover him, Johnson simply replied, "There is no best way to stop what I do."

Making the Grade

Johnson was born in Miami, Florida. He attended Miami Beach High School, where his talents on the football field were seen by many college scouts. Unfortunately, Chad's grades were not good enough to get him into a major college. It took some tough years for him to deal with his academic problems. Eventually,

Chad takes a well-deserved breather on the sideline during a game against the Detroit Lions.

Johnson's hard work was rewarded when he was given a scholarship to play at Oregon State University.

Oregon State

Johnson put up stellar numbers at Oregon State. In the 2000 season, he averaged 21.8 yards (20 m) per catch. Chad helped Oregon to a Fiesta Bowl victory over Notre Dame. Johnson finished the 2000 season with 37 catches for 806 yards (737 m) and 8 touchdowns. In the 2001 NFL draft, Chad was chosen by the Cincinnati Bengals.

Player Stats

Chad Johnson

Team: Cincinnati Bengals

Position: Wide Receiver

Height: 6' 1"

Weight: 192 lbs.

Born: 1/9/1978

College: Oregon State

NFL Experience: 5 years

Chad gets pulled down by Minnesota Vikings linebacker Dontarrious Thomas after picking up big yardage.

In the Spotlight

Since coming into the league, Johnson has developed into a touchdown scoring machine. He scored 9 touchdowns in 2005. Chad has also developed a taste for creative touchdown celebrations. In one game, Chad danced an Irish jig after a touchdown catch. While some people find Johnson's antics over the top, his popularity is undeniable.

Chapter Five

Brian Urlacher

Many people consider Brian Urlacher the best defensive player on the best defense in the NFL. His rare combination of size and speed makes him a multi-talented linebacker. He can rush the quarterback as well as cover a speedy wide receiver across the middle. Urlacher is the first Chicago defender to lead his team in tackles during his first four seasons. He is also one of only five players in the history of the league to be named to the Pro Bowl in each of his first four seasons.

Growing Up Urlacher

Brian was born in Pasco, Washington. From Pasco, he moved with his mother to Albuquerque where he discovered his talent for playing football. Brian played organized football at Lovington High School. He led his team to a perfect 14-0 record and a state title, playing both offense and defense.

Brian is all smiles after a 17-9 victory over the San Francisco 49ers.

Brian played college ball at the University of New Mexico (UNM). At UNM, Brian played outside linebacker and safety. He also played wide receiver on offense and returned kickoffs and punts. Urlacher finished his college career as the school's third highest tackler with 442 tackles.

Going Pro

Brian was drafted as the ninth overall pick in the 2000 NFL draft by Chicago, where he took the position of middle linebacker. His speed, aggression, and intelligence quickly brought

Player Stats

Brian Urlacher

Team: Chicago Bears

Position: Middle Linebacker

Height: 6' 4"

Weight: 258 lbs.

Born: 5/25/1978

College: University of New Mexico

NFL Experience: 6 years

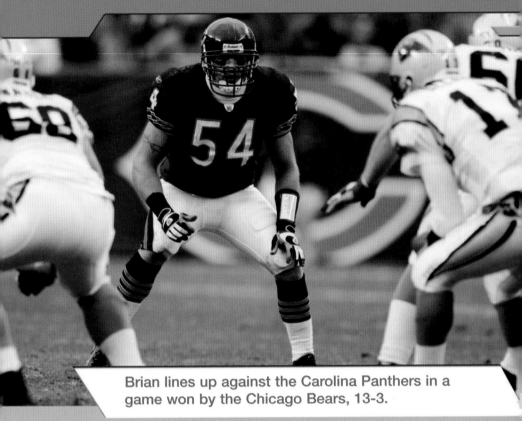

Brian lines up against the Carolina Panthers in a game won by the Chicago Bears, 13-3.

him stardom. Urlacher really enjoys playing football in Chicago. "The city is known for great defensive football teams," says Urlacher. Urlacher continues the Bears' tradition of excellent linebackers, following in the footsteps of George Connor, Dick Butkus, and Mike Singletary. In his first season, Urlacher was named the 2000 Defensive Rookie of the Year. Urlacher was also named the 2005 NFL Defensive Player of the Year.

Chapter Six

Peyton Manning

Many people rate Peyton Manning as the NFL's top quarterback. He was selected the first overall pick in the 1998 draft. Peyton has a strong arm and nearly perfect mechanics. In 2004, he had one of the greatest seasons ever by a quarterback. Peyton passed for 4,557 yards (4,166 m) and had a quarterback rating of 121.1. His 49 touchdown passes set a new NFL season record. Peyton's performance earned him the 2004 NFL MVP award.

Peyton's Youth

Peyton Manning was born in 1976 in New Orleans, Louisiana. His father, Archie Manning, was a football star at the University of Mississippi and in the NFL. Peyton played high school football in New Orleans and was one of the most highly recruited quarterbacks ever. Many people thought that Peyton would play at Mississippi, where his father had played.

Peyton sets up and looks to pass to an open receiver in a game against the Seattle Seahawks.

Peyton decided to play for the University of Tennessee instead, which was a move that shocked many people.

College Days

Peyton was a superstar at Tennessee. He is Tennessee's all-time leading passer with 11,201 yards (10,242 m) and 89 touchdowns. Although he completed his degree in three years, Peyton returned to Tennessee for his senior season in the hopes of winning a

Player Stats

Peyton Manning

Team: Indianapolis Colts

Position: Quarterback

Height: 6' 5"

Weight: 230 lbs.

Born: 3/24/1976

College: University of Tennessee

NFL Experience: 8 years

national championship. His hopes were dashed, however. Tennessee failed to beat arch-rival University of Florida.

The Professional

Since being drafted, Peyton has spent his entire NFL career with the Indianapolis Colts. In 2004, Manning signed a contract for $99.2 million. This made Peyton the highest-paid player in the NFL at the time. Many people agree that his talents make him worth the money. He runs the Indianapolis offense with great skill. After Peyton sees the defensive alignment, he will often call an audible, switching the play to take advantage. Although he has not won a Super Bowl, most agree that Peyton is one of the finest quarterbacks to ever play football.

The Brothers Manning

Peyton's younger brother, Eli, is also a quarterback in the NFL. Eli plays for the New

York Giants. So far, Eli has shown great talent as a quarterback, following in the Manning family tradition. Peyton and Eli talk to each other twice a week. During their chats, Peyton sometimes gives his younger brother advice based on his longer experience as a top quarterback in the NFL.

Older brother Peyton is proud of his kid brother. "People always ask me who my favorite player is," says Peyton. "I always say it's my little brother."

Sports Trivia

Starting the Super Bowl

The Super Bowl was originally called the AFL and NFL World Championship Game. The first such game was held in January 1967. In 1969, the name of the game was changed to the Super Bowl. The term was coined by Kansas City Chiefs' owner, Lamar Hunt.

Peyton calls out signals at the line of scrimmage in a 2005 playoff game against the Pittsburgh Steelers.

"Pey" It Back

Peyton believes in giving back to his community. He said, "With the great advantages of being an NFL quarterback comes great responsibility to make a difference in the community." Peyton set up the PeyBack Foundation, which contributes money to youth organizations in Indiana, Tennessee, and Louisiana. Peyton also helped to organize a Hurricane Katrina relief effort with his brother Eli.

There are many young NFL players with amazing skills, too. Although these players have only played professionally for one or two years, their talents are undeniable. Here are just a few of those who will become tomorrow's stars.

Ben Roethlisberger is one of the tallest quarterbacks in the league. Standing at 6' 5", he's not called "Big Ben" for nothing. He was drafted in 2004 by the Pittsburgh Steelers. When the Steelers' starting quarterback, Tommy Maddox, was injured in the second game of the season, Ben was called to action. He did not lose a game for the rest of the regular season. His teammates had confidence in Ben's abilities despite his being a rookie. Fellow Steeler Alan Faneca said, "He's definitely in the game and has control of it." Ben was named Rookie of the Year that year. The next year, Roethlisberger led the Steelers

Ben holds the Vince Lombardi Trophy, awarded to the winning team of the Super Bowl. Ben led the Pittsburgh Steelers to a 21-10 victory over the Seattle Seahawks to win Super Bowl XL in 2006.

to a Super Bowl win. He even scored the first touchdown of the game. At twenty-three years old, Ben became the youngest quarterback to ever win a Super Bowl.

Lofa Tatupu is another new player with great promise. Lofa's father, Mosi Tatupu, was a talented NFL player and Lofa is following in his footsteps. Lofa was selected in the second round of the NFL draft. He was the second-highest picked linebacker to ever have been chosen in the draft. He started all 18 games in 2005 with the Seattle Seahawks.

Lofa was the first rookie in twenty-eight years to lead the team with 105 tackles. Lofa is modest, though. Of his great rookie successes, he says, "Situation, circumstances, they worked well for me and I'm just happy to be here." His Seahawk teammates are happy he's there, too. Many list him as a major reason that the Seahawks made it to the Super Bowl in 2006.

Lofa tries to pick off a pass in a game against the Tennessee Titans.

New Words

audible (**aw**-duh-buhl) when a quarterback changes a play at the line of scrimmage

blitz (**blihtz**) when the quarterback is rushed by the opposing defensive players

contract (**kon**-trakt) an agreement between a team and a player that guarantees the amount of money a player will earn

forced fumbles (**forsd fuhm**-buhlz) when a defensive player makes an offensive player drop the football

Heisman Trophy (**hyz**-man **troh**-fee) an award given each year to the best college football player in the country

NFL draft (**en ef el draft**) an event where new players are chosen by teams. Only players who have been out of high school for three years or more can be chosen in the draft

PARADE All-American (puh-**rade awl** uh-**mer**-uh-kuhn) an award given to the best high school or college football players in the country each year

New Words

Pro Bowl (**pro bohl**) a game held at the end of a football season in which the top players from the AFC and NFC play against one another

quarterback rating (**kwor**-tur-bak **rayt**-ing) a system of rating passers, using statistics based on pass attempts, yards per pass attempt, percentage of touchdowns per attempt, and percentage of interceptions per attempt; ratings of more than 100 are exceptional

rookie (**ruk**-ee) an athlete who is in his first season with a team

sack (**sak**) tackling the quarterback behind the line of scrimmage.

scout (**skout**) someone sent to find out and bring back information

single coverage (**sing**-guhl **kuhv**-er-ij) when one offensive player is covered by one defensive player

For Further Reading

Preller, James. *NFL Reader: Rising Stars*. New York: Scholastic Inc., 2005.

Savage, Jeff. *Play by Play Football*. Minneapolis: LernerSports, 2003.

Stewart, Mark. *Peyton Manning: Rising Son*. Brookfield, CT: Millbrook Press, 2000.

Sumner, Jim. *Brian Urlacher: Windy City Warrior*. Champaign, IL: Sports Publishing, 2002.

Worthington, J.A. *The Mannings: Football's Famous Family*. Bloomington, MN: Red Brick Learning, 2005.

Resources

ORGANIZATIONS

Pro Football Hall of Fame
2121 George Halas Drive NW
Canton, Ohio 44708
Phone: (330) 456-8207
www.profootballhof.com

Youth Football USA
170 Forest Avenue
Fairfield, CT 06824
www.yfusa.org/

Resources

WEB SITES

American Youth Football: Games
www.americanyouthfootball.com/games.asp
Play football-themed online games on this Web site and follow the links to learn more about youth football in America.

The Official NFL Site for Kids
www.playfootball.com/
This Web site has football facts, online games, and links to kids' team pages.

Sports Illustrated for Kids: Football
www.sikids.com/football/index.html
See exciting photos and video of your favorite teams and players and learn cool football trivia on this Web site.

Index

Index

ABOUT THE AUTHOR

Virginia Buckman has written numerous books on a wide variety of nonfiction subjects. She currently lives and works in New York City.